The Sun

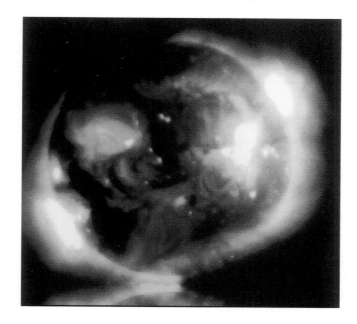

Mason Crest
450 Parkway Drive, Suite D
Broomall, PA 19008
www.masoncrest.com

© 2017 by Mason Crest, an imprint of National Highlights, Inc. All rights reserved.
No part of this publication may be reproduced or transmitted in any form or by any
means, electronic or mechanical, including photocopying, recording, taping, or
any information storage and retrieval system, without permission from the publisher.

Printed and bound in the United States of America.

First printing
9 8 7 6 5 4 3 2 1
Series ISBN: 978-1-4222-3547-8
ISBN: 978-1-4222-3553-9
ebook ISBN: 978-1-4222-8373-8

Library of Congress Cataologing-in-Publication is on file with the publisher.

THE SOLAR SYSTEM

Comets and Meteors • Far Planets • Giant Planets • Near Planets
Our Home Planet • Space Exploration • The Sun

KEY ICONS TO LOOK FOR:

 EDUCATIONAL VIDEOS: Readers can view videos by scanning our QR codes, providing them with additional educational content to supplement the text. Examples include news coverage, moments in history, speeches, iconic sports moments and much more!

 WORDS TO UNDERSTAND: These words with their easy-to-understand definitions will increase the reader's understanding of the text while building vocabulary skills.

Contents

Introduction

This book takes a close look at the body that breathes life into our world—the Sun. Day after day it pours heat and light on to the Earth. This makes the Earth warm and colorful, and a comfortable home for countless numbers of living things.

The Sun appears to travel around the Earth, but in fact the opposite is true. The Earth travels around the Sun. So do the other planets.

The Sun lies at the center of a great collection of circling bodies that we call the Solar System. They were all born together nearly 5,000 million years ago out of a vast cloud of gas and dust that once existed in our part of space.

The Sun is quite different from the other bodies in the Solar System. They are made up of rock, ice or cold gas, but the Sun is a globe of searing hot gases. If we could travel to the stars, we would find that they look like the Sun. We can think of the Sun as our daytime star.

△ Minutes before the Sun rises, it lights up the eastern sky.

Earth's orbit

Sun

Earth spins round

△ On the side of the Earth facing t[h]e Sun, it is daytime[.] On the side facing away, it is night.

Sun Time

The Sun provides us with a regular pattern of day and night.

Early in the morning, if you look to the east, you can see the Sun rise above the horizon. By midday it reaches its highest point, and then it starts descending. In the evening the Sun sets below the western horizon.

The following morning the Sun reappears over the eastern horizon and brings daylight once more. This regular cycle of day and night gives us our basic unit of time, the **day**. It is properly called the **solar** day, or the day according to the Sun. Shorter periods of time are measured by splitting the day into 24 hours, each hour into 60 minutes, and each minute into 60 seconds.

▽ In northern Norway in winter, the Sun never sets. That is why Norway is known as the land of the midnight Sun.

Earth's rotation

The Sun does not really circle the Earth every day. It only appears to. The Earth rotates, or spins, in space once a day, moving towards the east. This makes the Sun appear to move towards the west.

◁ An unusual sundial at Herstmonceux Castle, England. The position of the shadow on the circular ring gives the time.

The solar year

The Earth not only spins round in space. It also travels bodily through space in orbit around the Sun. It travels once around the Sun in 365¼ days. This period of time is called the **year**, or solar year. The **calendar** used in most countries is based on the solar year. But it is usually 365 days long. To make up for the extra ¼ day of the solar year, an extra day is added to the calendar year every four years. This is known as a **leap year**, and the extra day becomes February 29.

Among the stars

We know that the Earth circles in space around the Sun. But from the Earth it seems that the Sun circles the Earth. The Sun appears to travel through different **constellations** of stars. It follows the same path each year, called the **ecliptic**.

The Changing Seasons

The Earth spins on its **axis** as it circles the Sun. But the Earth's axis is not upright in relation to its **orbit**; it is tipped at an angle and stays pointing in the same direction in space all the time. This means that during the year the axis sometimes tips towards and sometimes away from the Sun.

The tipping axis causes a particular place on Earth to lean more towards the Sun at some times of the year than at others. The more it leans, the more heat it receives. This means that during the year the temperature at a place changes, bringing about changes in the weather, which we call the **seasons**.

Following the seasons

In the tropics above and below the **Equator**, there are only two seasons, a wet and a dry. But most of the world has four seasons: winter, spring, summer, and fall.

A place experiences winter when it is tilted furthest away from the Sun. In northern parts of the world, winter begins on December 21. As the Earth moves in its orbit, its axis shifts in relation to the Sun. Northern parts of the world start to tilt more towards the Sun and warm up.

summer Su

spring Su

The Sun is highest in summer and lowest in winter.

winter Sun

Δ **The beautiful colors of a forest in New England in the fall.**

northern spring

Earth

▷ Seasons take place because of the tilt of the Earth's axis. Places are warmer when they are tilted towards the Sun, and cooler when they are tilted away.

northern winter

northern summer

Sun

northern autumn

On March 21, spring begins. On this date the hours of daylight and darkness are the same all over the world. This is the spring, or vernal, **equinox** (meaning equal night).

Northern parts of the world continue heating up as they tilt more and more towards the Sun. On June 21, they are tilted most and summer begins. Then they start tilting away from the Sun and cooling down again. On about September 23, fall begins. This is the date of the autumnal equinox. Northern parts continue cooling down until winter returns again.

Seasons in Australia

The dates given here are for seasons in northern parts of the world, or in the northern hemisphere. In the southern hemisphere, the seasons are reversed because southern parts of the world are always tilted in the opposite direction from northern parts.

▷ Stonehenge, near Salisbury in southern England: Ancient Britons built this monument to follow the seasons.

Weather and Climate

Energy from the Sun drives the world's weather systems.

Only a tiny fraction of the energy the Sun pours out into space—about one part in 2,000 million—reaches the Earth. This energy produces the general conditions of the air around us that we call the weather. The most important feature of the weather is the temperature. This depends mainly on the amount of energy the Sun's rays provide. They heat up the Earth's surface, which in turn heats up the air above it. When the air warms, it rises. This sets up currents in the **atmosphere** known as winds.

beams of sunlight

Equator

△ **The energy in a beam of sunlight spreads over a small area at the Equator, but over a bigger area elsewhere. This is why the Equator is warmer than elsewhere.**

▽ **Astronauts photographed this huge weather system above the Atlantic. It was a hurricane named Bonnie.**

From National Geographic, a primer on how the Solar System is arranged.

▷ **Cacti growing in the Arizona desert. These plants can stand up to the hot, dry desert climate.**

The water cycle

When the Sun's rays fall on seas and rivers, the water heats up and evaporates, or turns to vapor. The vapor mixes with the air and is carried away by the wind. As the air cools, the vapor turns back into drops of water, creating clouds. When the drops grow large, they fall from the clouds as rain or snow. The rain and snow find their way back into the rivers and seas, and the process starts again. This process, called the water cycle, helps determine what the weather is like.

Climate

A particular place on Earth has a similar weather pattern year after year. We call this usual weather pattern the **climate**. The main feature of climate is temperature. The Sun's rays do not carry the same amount of energy to every place on Earth. This is because the Earth is round and the Sun's rays fall on the surface at different angles in different places.

The nearness of the sea also affects climate. Water holds on to heat better than land, so places by the ocean or large bodies of water often have a milder climate than places inland.

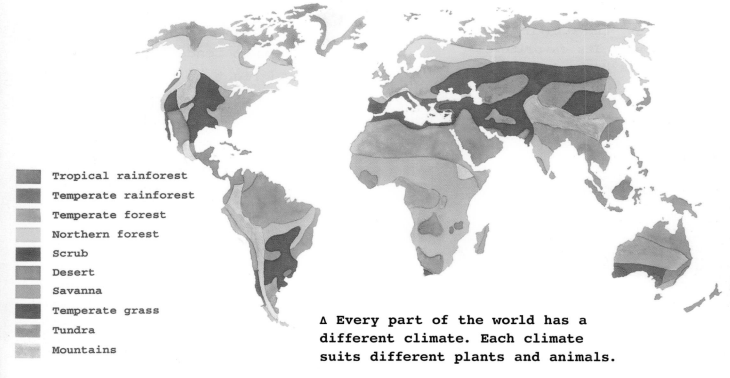

- ■ Tropical rainforest
- ■ Temperate rainforest
- ■ Temperate forest
- ■ Northern forest
- ■ Scrub
- ■ Desert
- ■ Savanna
- ■ Temperate grass
- ■ Tundra
- ■ Mountains

Δ **Every part of the world has a different climate. Each climate suits different plants and animals.**

Life from the Sun

The Sun's heat and light make Earth a comfortable home for living things.

The Earth is unique among the **planets** because it teems with life. A huge variety of different kinds, or species, of plants and animals live on the land, in the oceans, and in the air. Life forms vary in size from microscopic mites to gigantic whales bigger than a house. Most forms of life on our planet need warmth, water, and oxygen. They need warmth so that life-processes can take place in their bodies. They need water to carry substances around their bodies. And they must breathe the oxygen in the atmosphere to stay alive.

Just right

The Earth provides the warmth and water needed for life because it is in exactly the right position in the Solar System. If the Earth were closer to the Sun, all the water would evaporate and the temperature would be too high for living things. If the Earth were much further away from the Sun, it would be too cold for living things to thrive.

▽ **One of the Earth's tiny creatures, the 0.07-in (2mm) head louse. Its favorite habitat is human hair.**

Life protector
The Sun sends not only heat and light to the Earth, but also dangerous rays, such as ultraviolet (UV) rays. A layer of gas called ozone in the atmosphere blocks most UV rays, but pollution has caused the **ozone layer** to thin. If it becomes too thin, it will let through UV rays that could harm living things.

The green leaves
of plants make food
from carbon dioxide
and water.

Sun

carbon dioxide
from air

water
from roots

◁ The Moon
has no natural
life because
it has no
air or water.

leaf gives out oxygen

Light work

Besides warmth, water and oxygen, living
things also need food. Both animals and
plants need to consume food to produce
energy. They need energy to make their
bodies work and for growth and, in the
case of animals, movement. Animals
eat plants or other animals. They
cannot make their own food.

Plants can make their own food from
carbon dioxide gas and water. They take

in carbon dioxide from the atmosphere,
and water from the ground. The two
substances combine in a chemical
reaction in the plants' leaves to
make their food, sugar. But this process
takes place only in the daytime because
it needs the energy in sunlight to make it
work. That is why it is called **photosynthesis**,
which means making with light.

△ Sunscreen can protect
skin from invisible
ultraviolet rays.

◁ Alligators in one
of Florida's swamps
raise their
body temperature by
basking in the Sun.

13

Worshipping the Sun

Ancient peoples worshipped the Sun, which kept them warm and made their crops grow.

Sun worship dates back to the earliest civilizations, which grew up in the Middle and Far East. These civilizations developed after people began to farm for food around 8000 BCE. The early farming peoples worshipped the Sun because they realized how much they depended on sunshine to make their crops grow and ripen.

Sun worship was well established in the Middle East in Babylonia and Assyria and ancient Egypt by around 3000 BCE. We know this from the first written records from these civilizations. In ancient Egypt, the Sun god Ra became the most important figure.

Crossing the sky

In their mythology the Egyptians said that Ra sailed across the sky each day carrying the Sun in a sacred boat. During the night he sailed through the underworld, before rising into the sky again next day.

In ancient Chinese mythology, the Sun rode across the heavens in a chariot drawn by dragons. The ancient Greeks thought that their Sun god Helios drove across the sky in a horse-drawn chariot.

Later, in Ancient Greece, the god Apollo came to be recognized as a Sun god, although he was originally considered the god of light and purity.

▷ An Egyptian woman worships the Sun god, Ra, in a painting dating from about 1000 BCE. Ra is often depicted as a man with a falcon's head.

▲ Machu Picchu, the "lost city of the Incas" in the Andes mountains of South America.

Sacrifice for the Sun

Other people in the world continued to worship the Sun. Three great civilizations grew up in Central and South America that were obsessed by Sun worship. They were the Maya, the Inca, and the Aztecs. They flourished until the 1500s, when they were destroyed by invading Spaniards.

The Maya, Inca, and Aztecs all had powerful Sun gods, to whom they made regular sacrifices. The Aztecs carried out ceremonies to the Sun-god Huitzilopochtli. They believed that he would die and the Sun cease to shine unless he was fed each day with human blood and hearts. Sometimes thousands of people were sacrificed at the same ceremony.

Sun-day

In ancient Rome in about 270, the Emperor Aurelian decided that worship of the Sun would be the state religion. This continued until the Emperor Constantine adopted Christianity 50 years later. But the idea of Sun worship was not lost, for he gave the name Sunday to a weekly day of rest and prayer.

▲ Aztecs sacrificing captured prisoners at a pyramid temple: The main temple was a pyramid named Tenochtitlan. It was on the site of present-day Mexico city.

Studying the Sun

Astronomers study the Sun with special telescopes from the ground and from space.

The Sun is too bright to be looked at through an ordinary telescope. So **astronomers** build telescopes that project, or throw, an image of the Sun on to a screen, like a slide projector. There it can be studied and photographed. Most solar telescopes use sets of mirrors and lenses, mounted in a tall tower. A mirror on top of the tower, called a heliostat, reflects light from the Sun down a central tube. It turns during the day to follow the Sun's movement through the sky. The sunlight is brought to a focus on a table or screen in an observation room at the foot of the tower.

△ **The Sun's outer atmosphere, pictured by the <u>satellite</u> Solar Max**

▷ **The McMath solar telescope, at Kitt Peak Observatory in Arizona, is one of the world's biggest.**

Sun

heliostat

mirror

observation room

mirror

◁ **How the McMath telescope works.**

Sunlight is also studied using other instruments, including a spectrograph. This produces a colored **spectrum**, which shows what the Sun is made of (see page 25).

Looking at the atmosphere

Astronomers can study sunspots and other features of the Sun with solar telescopes. But they cannot study the Sun's fainter outer layers, or atmosphere. These layers become visible on Earth only during a **total eclipse** of the Sun, when the glaring surface is blotted out (see page 32).

But astronomers can use an instrument called a **coronagraph** to create an artificial eclipse. Then they can see eruptions in the Sun's atmosphere without having to wait for a real eclipse to occur.

WARNING!
Never look at the Sun with a telescope or binoculars. It is so bright that it will damage your eyes and may even blind you.

Seeing the invisible

The Sun puts out many other kinds of rays besides light, such as X-rays and radio waves (see page 24). Radio waves can be studied from the ground using radio telescopes. But X-rays cannot be studied because they do not pass through the Earth's atmosphere. To study X-rays, astronomers send instruments into space on spacecraft. Space instruments can also study other radiation from the Sun that is blocked by the atmosphere, such as gamma rays and ultraviolet rays. The other great advantage of using instruments in space is that they can view the Sun more clearly and for a longer time.

Daytime Star

The Sun is like the other stars we see in the night sky, but much closer to us.

If we could travel into space and look at the Sun, we would find that it looks just like a star. For that is what the Sun is, an ordinary star.

From the Earth, the Sun looks larger and brighter than the other stars only because it is much closer to us. On average, it lies about 93 million miles (150 million km) away. The next closest star, called Proximo Centauri, lies more than 4.2 **light-years** away.

∇ **The Sun belongs to a galaxy (below), along with billions of other stars, like these in the constellation Cygnus (left).**

Enormous size

With a diameter of some 864,000 miles (1.4 million km), the Sun is huge compared with the Earth. It could swallow more than one million bodies the size of the Earth, and it has more than 300,000 times the Earth's mass. But, compared with many stars, the Sun is tiny. Astronomers know of stars that are hundreds of times bigger.

So they call the Sun a dwarf star. In fact they call it a yellow dwarf because of the color of the light it gives off.

The Sun is the same temperature as other yellow stars, about 10,000°F (5500°C). This is the temperature of the Sun's surface. It is much hotter inside (see page 20).

The Sun is really quite a small star. Stars called giants are tens of times bigger, and supergiants are tens of times bigger still.

Red dwarf

Sun

Make-up

Like all the other stars, the Sun is a ball of very hot, glowing gas. The two main gases are hydrogen and helium. These are the two lightest basic substances, or **chemical elements**. The Sun also contains traces of many heavier elements, including carbon, iron, silicon, and magnesium. Altogether, 70 different elements have been found in the Sun.

Sun in the Universe
The Sun is one of about 100,000 million stars that form a star island, or galaxy, in space. This galaxy is one of a group, or cluster, of galaxies in our corner of space. Millions of clusters of galaxies make up the Universe.

The Sun's movement

Like the Earth, the Sun moves in two ways. It spins round on its axis and it travels bodily through space. We can see how the Sun spins by watching the dark specks called **sunspots** on its surface. Near the Equator, the Sun spins round once in about 25 days. Near the poles, it takes more than a month to turn round once. The Sun also travels in a long path, or orbit, around the center of our galaxy. It takes about 225 million years to go full circle. We call this period of time a **cosmic year**.

Famed scientist Stephen Hawking talks about the formation of the Solar System.

White giant

Red giant

Supergiant

Inside the Sun

Nuclear reactions produce the energy that keeps the sun shining.

Years ago, people thought that the Sun was a great ball of fire. But if it was, it would burn out in only a few thousand years. Astronomers believe that the Sun has been shining for nearly 5000 million years. And they think it will carry on shining for another 5000 million years.

To find out how the Sun produces its enormous energy we must look deep inside it, into its center, or core. In this region, hundreds of thousands of miles below the surface, pressures are enormous.

▽ **Energy produced in the Sun's core travels as radiation to the convection zone. In this zone, currents of gas carry the energy to the surface, or photosphere.**

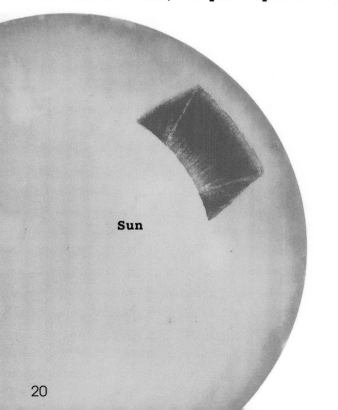

photosphere

convection zone

radiation zone

core

Sun

Temperatures in the core are also incredibly high: 270 million°F (15 million °C) or more. At such temperatures, the gas hydrogen takes part in processes, or **reactions**, that produce enormous energy.

Nuclear reactions

On Earth, hydrogen exists as atoms, like all other chemical elements. Each atom is made up of two tiny particles. There is a proton in the center, or nucleus, of the atom, and an electron circling around it. In the searing heat of the Sun, hydrogen does not exist as atoms. It is just a mixture

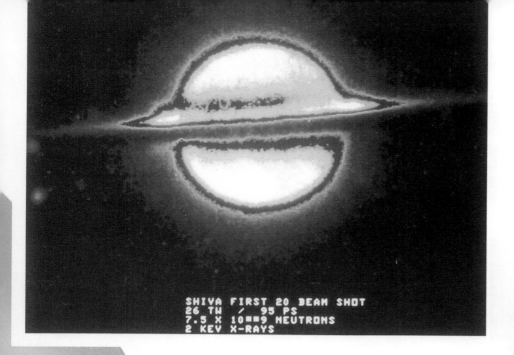

SHIVA FIRST 20 BEAM SHOT
26 TH   /   95 PS
7.5 X 10■■9 NEUTRONS
2 KEV X-RAYS

△ **A bright flash of energy given out in a nuclear fusion experiment carried out in a laboratory.**

▽ **This stained glass window honors Albert Einstein, who devised the famous equation $E = mc^2$. It is in Grace Cathedral, San Francisco.**

of protons and electrons. Because of the heat these particles are moving around at very high speeds, Often they collide. Sometimes protons hit one another and stick together to form larger groups of particles. These groups are the centers of another chemical element called helium. We call this sticking-together process **fusion**, or nuclear fusion because the protons are particles from the nuclei (centers) of hydrogen atoms.

Matter into energy

When nuclear fusion takes place, an enormous amount of energy is given out. This happens because a certain amount of matter taking part in the process is changed into energy. The scientist Albert Einstein was the first person to explain that such a change can occur. Every second in the Sun, 4,000,000 tons of matter are converted into energy.

$E = mc^2$
Einstein's famous equation $E = mc^2$ explains how nuclear fusion produces huge amounts of energy. E is the energy produced when mass (m) is converted into energy; c is the speed of light. Because light travels very fast, c^2 is an enormous quantity. This means that E must be enormous, too.

The Sun's Face

Dark spots often appear on the bright, bubbling surface of the Sun.

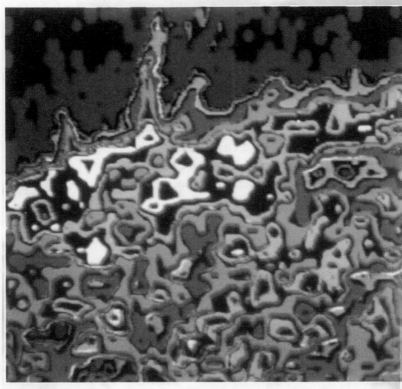

◁ **This photograph (with colors added) shows slight differences in brightness on the Sun.**

The face of the Sun that we see is known as the **photosphere**, meaning light-sphere. It is the part that gives off the energy the Sun produces inside its core as heat, light, and other kinds of radiation (see page 24). The temperature of the photosphere is about 9900°F (5500°C).

The photosphere is a layer about 300 miles (500 km) thick. Close-up photographs show that it is made up of boiling gases. They give the surface of the Sun a grainy appearance, which astronomers call granulation. In each granule, hot gas from below rises, gives off heat and then sinks as it cools.This process is called convection.

The whole photosphere moves up and down about 15 miles (25 km) every five minutes. Other stars vibrate in much the same way. Some change in size so much that their brightness varies noticeably. We call them variable stars.

Spots on the Sun

The photosphere is not the same all over. Particularly bright spots occur here and there. And dark blotches called sunspots appear from time to time.

The sunspot cycle

Sunspots come and go over a period of about 11 years. This is called the sunspot, or solar, cycle. At the beginning of the cycle, hardly any sunspots are found. Then, year by year, sunspot numbers increase to a maximum before falling again.

Sunspots occur in regions where the Sun's magnetism is intense—thousands of times stronger than the Earth's magnetism. This magnetism triggers off all kinds of activity in the atmosphere above (see page 28).

▷ **Regions of strong magnetism are found around sunspots.**

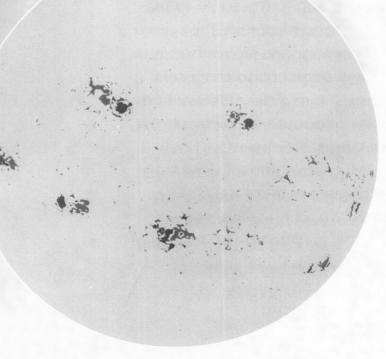

Sunspots look like ink blots on blotting paper. They look dark because they are cooler than the surrounding surface. On average, their temperature is about 2700°F (1500°C) lower.

Usually, sunspots appear in groups, with two main spots. They vary widely in size. Some may measure only a few hundred miles across, but others may be bigger than the Earth. The large ones may remain visible for months at a time.

▽ **The butterfly diagram, a pattern that shows how the position of sunspots changes year by year (see Solar butterflies box above).**

The Sun's Rays

The Sun pours out its energy as light and heat, and also as rays we cannot see or feel.

The Earth is alive because of the energy it receives from the Sun. Most of this energy comes to us in the form of light and heat. We can detect light rays with our eyes, and feel heat rays with our bodies. But the Sun also gives out energy in the form of rays, or radiation, that our bodies cannot detect. These rays include gamma rays, X-rays, ultraviolet rays and radio waves.

These rays belong to the same family of rays as light and heat rays. They are called electromagnetic waves because they are tiny electrical and magnetic disturbances. The rays are different from one another because their waves have a different length. Gamma rays have the shortest wavelengths: it would take a billion of them to measure a yard. Radio waves have the longest wavelengths: they can be up to several miles long. All these rays travel at the speed of light: 186,000 miles (300,000 kilometers) per second.

The Sun's dark lines
When astronomers look closely at the spectrum of sunlight, they find it is criss-crossed by hundreds of dark lines. By studying these spectral lines, they can tell what the Sun is made of. Different sets of lines are produced by the different chemical elements in the Sun.

Visible light

Ultraviolet rays

X-rays

Gamma rays

△ A beautiful rainbow lights up a stormy sky.

Looking at light

The light that comes from the Sun appears white, but it is not really white at all. We can see this if we pass a narrow beam of light into a wedge, or prism, of glass. The light that comes out is made up of different colors, called a spectrum. Each color is light of a different wavelength. We often see the same colors in a rainbow. They are produced when sunlight is split into different wavelengths when it passes through raindrops. The main colors in the spectrum are violet, indigo, blue, green, yellow, orange, and red.

▷ This picture of the Sun has been taken using the X-rays it gives out. The bright areas show hot regions in the Sun's atmosphere.

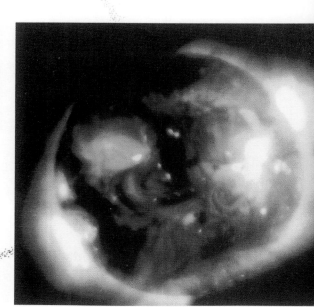

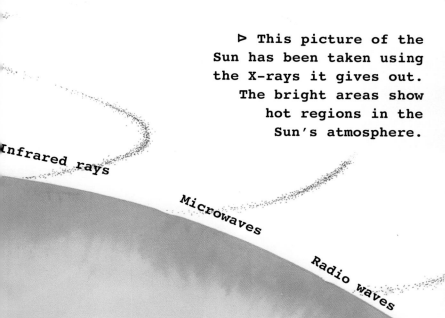

Infrared rays

Microwaves

Radio waves

Solar Power

We can harness the Sun's energy for heating and making electricity.

The Sun pours down on the Earth more energy than the world will ever need. In only an hour, it supplies more energy than the human population uses in a year. The problem is that this solar energy is spread out over a large area and is difficult, and often expensive, to harness on a large scale.

But many houses in warm climates do use solar power for heating water. And solar power stations make electricity for household use.

▽ **This tiny vehicle is a solar-powered car called Sunraycer. Its batteries are kept charged by electricity produced by solar panels.**

Solar collectors

Houses that use solar heating generally use flat-plate collectors to harness the Sun's heat. They consist of a flat box covered with a plate of glass. Sunlight passes through the glass into the box and heats up water in a coil inside. The warm water is piped to the house's hot-water heater.

Solar power stations use hundreds of mirror-like reflectors to concentrate the Sun's rays. Some reflect the rays on to a central tower, where they heat up a liquid that carries the heat to a boiler. The boiler produces steam to drive electricity generators.

Other systems use curved reflectors that heat liquid in tubes suspended above them. One power plant of this type is in the sunny Mojave Desert in California. It uses 650,000 mirrors spread over two square miles (five square kilometers).

▷ **Some of the hundreds of thousands of mirrors at a solar power station in the Mojave Desert, California.**

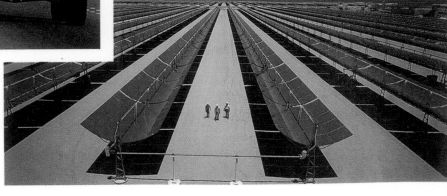

▷ This is the kind of solar panel used to heat water in houses. The glass-topped panel traps the heat of the Sun. Water inside the copper coil transfers the heat to the hot-water heater that supplies the house.

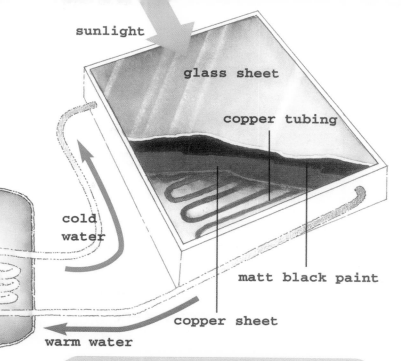

sunlight

glass sheet

copper tubing

matt black paint

copper sheet

cold water

warm water

house hot-water cylinder

Solar cells

Spacecraft use electronic devices called **solar cells** to harness the Sun's energy. Solar cells produce electricity when sunlight falls on them. They are made of the same material as the microchips in computers: crystals of silicon. A single solar cell is only a few inches wide and produces a tiny amount of electricity. Spacecraft are fitted with large panels made up of thousands of cells to produce enough electricity.

Satellite power stations
In about 20 years time, huge power stations may be circling in orbit 22,000 miles (36,000 km) above the Earth. They will always be in the sunlight and will produce power using panels of solar cells. The solar energy will be beamed down to Earth, where it will be converted to electricity and fed into the power lines.

◁ The solar panels on the Hubble Space Telescope produce enough electricity to power Hubble's instruments and radio equipment.

The Stormy Atmosphere

Dazzling flares and fiery fountains constantly spring up in the Sun's stormy atmosphere.

Above the Sun's hot, spotty surface, or photosphere, there are layers of gases, which make up the Sun's atmosphere. There are two layers of atmosphere. The one nearest the Sun is called the **chromosphere**, or color sphere, because it is pinkish in color. The outer atmosphere is called the **corona**, which means crown.

See video of solar flares and the radiation from a massive solar storm.

◁ A tongue of fire, called a solar prominence, shoots out from the Sun. In an hour, it has traveled hundreds of thousands of miles into space.

Inside the atmosphere

The Sun's atmosphere is visible only during a total eclipse of the Sun, when the Moon briefly blots out the surface of the Sun. The chromosphere is about 6,200 miles (10,000 km) deep. Its lower part is cooler than the photosphere, but the temperature rises the higher up you go. The gas in the chromosphere becomes thinner higher up, too. In the corona, the atmosphere carries on thinning until it merges into empty space. But this does not happen for millions of miles. The corona is incredibly hot, with temperatures as high as 2,000,000°C.

The Skylab project
Studying the Sun was one of the main objects of the Skylab project in the 1970s. Astronauts aboard the US space station took more than 150,000 images using eight solar telescopes and revealed a Sun no one had ever seen before. The International Space Station continues this work today.

▽ **Loops of hot gas surge through the Sun's corona. This picture was taken by the coronagraph on the SOHO probe. The disc in the center of the picture blots out the glaring face of the Sun.**

The lively chromosphere

In the chromosphere, flame-like jets of gases, called spicules, burst through from the photosphere all the time. But the action really heats up when sunspots appear in the photosphere below. The invisible lines of magnetic force found around sunspots carry gases from the chromosphere into the corona. These bursts of hot gas are called prominences. They appear as fiery fountains or great flaming arches.

Solar flare-up

The most violent activities taking place in the chromosphere are solar **flares**. These are explosions that take place without warning, usually around newly formed sunspots. They appear to be the sudden release of magnetic energy. When a solar flare erupts, it is the brightest feature on the Sun.

◁ **The brilliant white corona flashes into view briefly during a total eclipse of the Sun. In the corona, temperatures can rise as high as 2,000,000°C.**

The Solar Wind

Streams of particles flow out from the Sun, creating a kind of solar wind.

The Sun not only gives off radiation, such as heat and light, it also gives off masses of tiny particles. They are known as charged particles because they carry tiny amounts, or charges, of electricity. The most common kinds of particles are protons and electrons. These are the particles that are found in the atoms of all substances.

The charged particles escape from the Sun, travel through its atmosphere and then flow out into space in a stream called the **solar wind**. The wind flows out into space in all directions, eventually reaching the outermost regions of the Solar System.

Particles in the solar wind become trapped by Earth's magnetism to form radiation belts.

Van Allen radiation belts

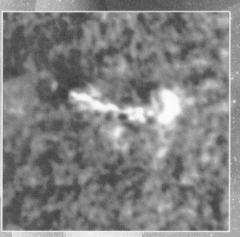

◁ **Solar flares like this make the solar wind blow strongly.**

Gale warnings

For much of the time, the solar wind blows gently, just like a summer breeze on Earth. It takes a week or more for the particles to reach the Earth. But the wind can be gusty, and may suddenly increase in strength to gale force, with the particles reaching the Earth in only about two days.

Wind effects

We cannot see the solar wind, but we can see the way it affects other things, such as comets. When a comet travels towards the Sun, it gives off clouds of gas and dust. The radiation given off by the Sun makes the gas particles electrically charged. When the solar wind blows, it sweeps the gas particles away from the head of the comet to form the comet's tail.

△ A brilliant display
of the Aurora Australis,
or southern lights,
seen from space.

Earth

△ The tail of the Comet
Ikeya—Seki lights up the
evening sky in 1965. It
was one of the brightest
comets of the century.

Earth's magnetic field

Colored lights

Normally, a kind of magnetic shield protects the Earth from the wind. But if the wind blows strongly, it can make charged particles enter the Earth's atmosphere and cause magnificent displays of colored lights, called the **aurora**. These displays are also known as the Northern Lights in northern parts of the world and the Southern Lights in southern parts.

Strong gusts in the solar wind can also affect the Earth's magnetism, causing what are called magnetic storms. When these storms happen, radio communications are upset, and electrical power supplies can be cut off.

The Sun in Eclipse

Sometimes the Moon covers the Sun and plunges the Earth into darkness.

The Sun, the Earth, and the Moon perform a complicated dance as they travel through space. The Moon whirls around the Earth, while the Earth whirls around the Sun. About once every 18 months or so, the Moon moves exactly into line between the Sun and the Earth and blots out the Sun's light. The Moon casts a dark shadow on the Earth and, for an instant, turns day into night. We call this a total **eclipse** of the Sun, or a solar eclipse.

The Moon is quite a small body, and casts quite a small shadow in space.

Its shadow only just touches the Earth during a total eclipse, and it never covers an area wider than 167 miles (270 km). Outside this area, people will see the Moon only partly cover the Sun. This is a partial eclipse.

During a total solar eclipse, the Moon's shadow darkens part of the Earth. The surrounding regions have only a partial eclipse and remain light.

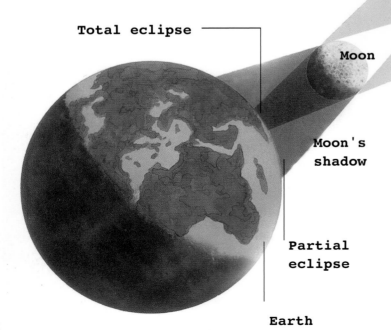

Total eclipse

Moon

Moon's shadow

Partial eclipse

Earth

Eclipse watching

A total eclipse of the Sun is a spectacular sight. It is a weird experience to find night falling in the middle of the day! Animals find it confusing, too. Astronomers travel all over the world to see total eclipses for another reason. It is only during an eclipse that they can see the Sun's atmosphere. Usually, it is masked by the glaring surface of the Sun.

Four stages of a total eclipse of the Sun

An eclipse begins when the Moon first starts to move over the Sun's surface. It takes about an hour to cover it. Then darkness descends. Around the Moon, the Sun's pinkish inner atmosphere and perhaps even prominences come into view. The outer atmosphere, or corona, shows up like a milky white crown. But soon the Sun emerges from behind the Moon, and daylight returns to the Earth. An eclipse does not last long. This is because the shadow moves rapidly over the Earth as the Sun moves behind the Moon. The longest a total eclipse can last is about 7½ minutes, but most eclipses are much shorter.

The curious coincidence

A total eclipse of the Sun can take place because of a curious coincidence. In diameter, the Sun is about 400 times bigger than the Moon. But the Moon is about 400 times closer to us than the Sun. This means that the Moon appears to be about the same size as the Sun in the sky, and can cover it up completely.

1 The dark Moon slowly covers the face of the Sun.

2 Total eclipse: prominences appear around the edge of the Moon.

3 Total eclipse: the pearly white corona shows up brilliantly.

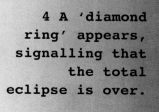

4 A 'diamond ring' appears, signalling that the total eclipse is over.

The Solar System

The Sun travels through space with a large family.

The Earth is one of eight planets that orbit in space around the Sun. The planets form the major part of the Sun's family in space, called the Solar System.

Circling the Sun

The planets circle around the Sun at different distances, in lengthy paths, or orbits. The planet nearest the Sun is Mercury, then in order come Venus, Earth, Mars, Jupiter, Saturn, Uranus, and Neptune.

The orbits of the planets are far apart, varying from tens of millions of miles in the inner part of the Solar System to thousands of millions of miles in the outer part. The planets are held in their orbits by the **gravity** of the Sun. This is so powerful that it can hold on to a ball of icy rock about 1367 miles (2200 km) wide over a distance of up to 4.67 billion miles (7.5 billion km). This ball is the dwarf planet Pluto.

The planets circle around the Sun in the same direction. If you could travel to a point in space far above the Earth's North Pole and look back, you would see the planets travelling anticlockwise. Most planets travel round the Sun in orbits that are nearly circular. But Mercury travels in orbits that are oval, or elliptical. All the planets travel around the Sun in much the same plane. This means that they and the Sun could be placed, more or less, on a flat sheet in space.

Uranus

Earth

Mercury

Saturn

Mars

Sun

Venus

Jupiter

comet

Neptune

Pluto

direction of planets

direction of planets

◁ **The orbits of the planets, drawn roughly to the same scale.**

▽ **Some of the smaller members of the Sun's family: Halley's comet (right) and four of the moons of Jupiter.**

Fellow travelers

Many other bodies belong to the Sun's family. Most of the planets have satellites, or **moons**, circling round them. Between the orbits of Mars and Jupiter there is a swarm of **asteroids**. They are rocky lumps, at most only a few hundred miles wide. Smaller still are the icy lumps we call comets.

Take a video tour with re-creations of the early moments of the Solar System.

Δ One of the many huge clouds of gas and dust that exist in space. It is found in the Eagle Nebula. Stars like the Sun are born in clouds like this.

Δ The Sun began to form when a cloud started to collapse under gravity. The shrinking cloud began to spin around and formed a flat disc shape.

Birth of the Solar System

The Solar System was born in a vast, billowing cloud of gas and dust.

Wisps of gas and tiny specks of dust are found everywhere in the space between the stars. They form interstellar matter. In some places they gather into enormous clouds millions and millions of miles wide. These clouds contain many different chemical substances, but the most common substance is the gas hydrogen.

There was once a huge cloud in space where the Solar System lies today. About 4,600 million years ago, the cloud began to collapse. Astronomers think that shock waves from a nearby exploding star caused this to happen. Inside the cloud, the particles of gas and dust were pulled together by gravity. At the same time the cloud began to swirl. This continued for thousands of years, with the cloud becoming smaller and flattening out into a disc. In the center of the disc, a ball of denser matter formed. It became very hot, and started to glow.

The infant Sun

The glowing center of the shrinking cloud was the infant Sun. As the infant Sun continued to shrink, the temperature inside it built up until it reached more than 10 million degrees. At this temperature, hydrogen atoms began to fuse (join) together to form helium atoms. Fantastic amounts of energy were released in this process, which is called **nuclear fusion**. For the first time, the Sun began to shine as a new star.

◁ A planetary nebula called the Stingray.

The planets

The particles in the disc of swirling gas and dust surrounding the Sun collided and stuck together. First they formed into larger lumps called planetesimals. These gradually clumped together to form the planets. Many lumps were left over, and these are what we now call asteroids and comets.

▽ At the center of the cloud, a ball of matter formed. It was the infant Sun.

Death of the Sun
In about 5,000 million years, the Sun will start to die. It will expand and turn red. Then its outer layers will blow away, leaving a small, hot core. The Sun will become a white dwarf star. But in time its light will fade. The Sun will end its life as a black dwarf.

▷ The infant Sun began to shine. Matter in the surrounding disc formed huge clumps.

▷▷ In time, the clumps swept up most of the matter around them. They became the planets.

Dwarfs and Giants

Earth is a medium-sized planet: three planets are smaller, four are larger.

There is no such thing as a typical planet. All the planets are different from one another in appearance, in make-up, and in size. To us, the Earth seems huge. Indeed, it is bigger than its neighbors in the inner part of the Solar System, Mercury, Venus, and Mars.

▽ The eight planets, drawn to the same scale. Jupiter and Saturn are by far the biggest. The Earth is tiny in comparison.

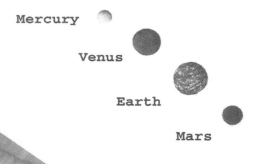

Mercury

Venus

Earth

Mars

Sun

These three planets are similar in composition to the Earth, being made up mainly of layers of rock on top of a center, or core, of metal. This is why they are called the terrestrial, or Earth-like planets.

The giants

The Earth may be bigger than its planetary neighbors, but it is tiny when compared with other planets further out. The two largest ones are Jupiter and Saturn, which lie far beyond Mars. They are truly giant-sized. Jupiter's diameter is 11 times that of the Earth, and Saturn is only slightly smaller. Together, these two planets

Saturn

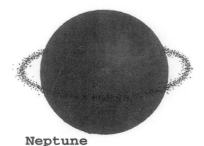

▲ Rocks litter the surface of Mars, one of the three Earth-like planets.

Uranus

Neptune

have more than 92 percent of the mass of all the planets put together. Uranus and Neptune are much smaller than Jupiter and Saturn, but still dwarf the Earth.

Gas balls

The four giant planets are made up mainly of gases, particularly hydrogen and helium, and they all have a very deep and very cold, gassy atmosphere. Beneath the atmosphere, there is an ocean of liquid gas. There is no solid surface at all. Beneath the ocean, the pressure is so great that the gas turns into liquid metal. Only at the very center of the planet is there a core of rock.

But the gas giants are dwarfed by the biggest body in the Solar System—the Sun. This is also a gas ball, of course, but it is made up of gas that is searing hot.

Moons and rings

There are other major differences between the dwarf terrestrial planets and the gas giants. The four terrestrial planets have between them only three satellites, or moons. The four giant planets have between them at least 64 moons! Another feature of the giant planets is that they all have systems of rings circling round them. Saturn has the broadest rings, easily visible from Earth through telescopes. None of the terrestrial planets has rings.

Planets in the Sky

The five closest planets often shine brightly in the night.

On many evenings of the year, a very bright star appears in the western sky just as the Sun sets. But this bright object, which is called the evening star, is not a star at all. It is the planet Venus. It shines so brightly because it is the closest planet to the Earth.

Of the near planets, Mercury and Saturn are usually difficult to see. Mercury is hard to spot because it never strays very far away from the Sun in the sky. It always appears very low down on the horizon and in a light sky. Saturn can be as bright as the brightest stars, but is hard to find unless you know exactly where to look.

Mars and Jupiter are usually easy to spot. They can both become much brighter than any star and shine like beacons in the night sky. You can easily tell them apart because Jupiter is a brilliant white, while Mars has a distinct reddish glow. That is why it is called the Red Planet.

▽ **The constellations of the zodiac, which astrologers call star signs. Most are named after animals.**

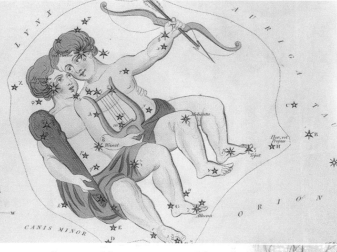

△ **The zodiac constellation Gemini, the Twins. Its twin bright stars are named Castor and Pollux.**

You can see four more planets in the night sky with the naked eye— Mercury, Mars, Jupiter, and Saturn. The remaining planets, Uranus and Neptune, are too faint to be visible because they are so far away.

◁ The star sign Cancer, illustrated in an old Turkish astrology book.

Among the stars

The planets do not appear just anywhere in the night sky. They can be found only in a narrow band passing through certain constellations. This band is called the **zodiac**. This name means the "circle of animals," because most of the constellations it passes through have animal names, such as Leo (Lion) and Taurus (Bull). Ancient star-gazers believed that the positions of the Sun and the planets in the zodiac affected people's characters and the lives they led. This belief was called **astrology**. Many people still believe in astrology, although astronomers have found no scientific evidence that there is any truth in it.

The evening star Venus appears with the crescent Moon in the western sky at sunset.

Time Line

2136 BCE
On October 22, Chinese astronomers make the first record of an eclipse of the Sun.

c 2000 BCE
Ancient Britons build Stonehenge, in present-day Wiltshire, as a kind of solar observatory. Stones are aligned to mark points on the horizon where the Sun rises and sets in different seasons, notably at midsummer and midwinter.

585 BCE
Thales of Miletus predicts the total eclipse of the Sun on May 28. The eclipse is so startling that it stops the war being fought between the Medes and the Lydians.

538 BCE
First record of a solar eclipse in England, described in the Anglo-Saxon Chronicles.

c 300 BCE
Aristarchus suggests that the Earth might circle around the Sun.

c CE 150
Ptolemy writes down all the astronomical knowledge and beliefs of the ancient world, including the idea that the Earth is the center of the Universe.

600s–1400s
The Mayan, Aztec, and Inca civilizations thrive in Central and South America. Sun worship is a major religion.

1600
Giordano Bruno is tortured and burned at the stake for believing in a Solar System, against the teachings of the Church.

1609
Johannes Kepler publishes the first of his three laws of planetary motion. It describes how the planets circle the Sun in elliptical not circular, orbits.

1610
Galileo first observes sunspots, using the new telescope he has built.

1666
Isaac Newton uses a prism to split white sunlight into a colored spectrum.

1781
William Herschel discovers a seventh planet, Uranus.

1796
Pierre Laplace puts forward his Nebular Hypothesis, suggesting that the Solar System was born in a cloud of gas in space.

1801
Giovanni Piazzi discovers the first and largest asteroid, Ceres.

1802
William Wollaston first observes the dark lines in the Sun's spectrum.

1814
Josef von Fraunhofer studies the dark lines in the Sun's spectrum, which come to be called Fraunhofer lines.

1836
Francis Baily first observes the "beads" of light around the Moon, just before total eclipse. They become known as Baily's beads.

1846
Johann Galle discovers the eighth planet, Neptune.

1889
George Hale invents the spectroheliograph, for detailed study of the Sun's spectrum.

1850
Heinrich Schwabe discovers the 11-year sunspot cycle.

1904
Edward Maunder draws the first butterfly diagram, showing how the location of sunspots changes over time.

1905
Albert Einstein introduces his Theory of Relativity, which includes his famous equation $E = mc^2$.

1908
George Hale measures the magnetic field of the Sun.

1919
Studies of the exceptionally long total solar eclipse on May 26 (6 minutes 50 seconds duration) in South America and Africa show that starlight is bent by the Sun's gravity. This effect was predicted by Albert Einstein's General Theory of Relativity (1916).

1930
Clyde Tombaugh discovers Pluto. Bernard Lyot invents the coronagraph.

1962
The world's largest solar telescope, the McMath, is completed at Kitt Peak National Observatory in Arizona.

1973
Skylab space station launched. Major objective is to study the Sun.

1995
SOHO probe launched to study the Sun. Discovers "sunquakes" and spots comets diving into the surface.

1999
Total solar eclipse visible across northern Europe and central and southern Asia on August 11.

2006
The International Astronomical Union declares that Pluto, once the ninth planet, is now considered one of several dwarf planets.

Sun data

Diameter at Equator	864,000 miles (1.4 million km)
Average distance from Earth	93 million miles (149 million km)
Volume (Earth's volume = 1)	1,304,000
Mass (Earth's mass = 1)	330,000
Density (water's density = 1)	1.4
Temperature on surface	9932°F (5500°C)
Temperature in center	27 million°F (15 million°C)
Spins on axis in	25 days
Star type	yellow dwarf (G2)
Circles round galaxy in	225,000,000 Earth-years
Distance from center of galaxy	25,000 light-years

Sun and the planets

Planet	Average distance from Sun million miles (million km)	Circles Sun in (d = Earth-days, y = Earth-years)
Mercury	36 (58)	88 d
Venus	67 (108.2)	224.7 d
Earth	93 (149.6)	365.25 d
Mars	141.6 (227.9)	687 d
Jupiter	483.6 (778.3)	11.9 y
Saturn	888 (1,427)	29.5 y
Uranus	1.8 (2,870)	84 y
Neptune	2.8 (4,497)	164.8 y

Size of the planets

Planet	Diameter at Equator: miles (km)	Volume (Earth's volume = 1)	Mass (Earth's mass = 1)
Mercury	3,031 (4,878)	0.05	0.06
Venus	7,521 (12,104)	0.82	0.88
Earth	7,962 (12,756)	1	1
Mars	4,221 (6,794)	0.15	0.11
Jupiter	88,358 (142,200)	1,320	318
Saturn	74,564 (120,000)	744	95
Uranus	31,814 (51,200)	67	15
Neptune	30,757 (49,500)	57	17

People file

Name	Nationality	Dates
Aristarchus	Greek	(310-230 BCE)
Francis Baily	English	(1774-1844)
Nicolaus Copernicus	Polish	(1473-1543)
Albert Einstein	German/US	(1879-1955)
Joseph von Fraunhofer	German	(1787-1826)
Galileo	Italian	(1564-1642)
Johann Galle	German	(1812-1910)
William Herschel	English	(1738-1822)
George Hale	US	(1868-1938)
Johannes Kepler	German	(1571-1630)
Pierre Laplace	French	(1749-1827)
Bernard Lyot	French	(1897-1953)
Edward Maunder	English	(1851-1928)
Isaac Newton	English	(1642-1727)
Giovanni Piazzi	Italian	(1746-1926)
Ptolemy	Greek	(c 150)
Heinrich Schwabe	German	(1789-1875)
Thales of Miletus	Greek	(c 640-560 BCE)
Clyde Tombaugh	US	(1906-1997)

AT THE SPEED OF LIGHT

Light from the Sun takes about 8½ minutes to reach the Earth, but over 4½ years to reach the nearest star.

ELEMENTARY

The Sun contains more than 70 out of the 100 or so elements found naturally on Earth.

DISCOVERY

The element helium was discovered in the Sun before it was discovered on Earth.

PASSING THROUGH

Every second, more than a billion particles called neutrinos, given off by the Sun, pass through our bodies without doing us any harm.

BLOWING A GALE

The solar wind streams away from the Sun at speeds of up to 1.86 million miles an hour.

MASSIVE

The Sun contains 99.9 percent of all the mass in the Solar System, totalling about 2000 million million million million tons.

SOME SPOT

The biggest sunspot ever was observed in April 1947, measuring about 186,000 miles long and 90,000 miles wide.

BURNING QUESTION

If the Sun were made up of glowing coal, it would burn itself out in 1,500 years.

FAST MOVER

The Sun hurtles through space at a speed of about 155 miles (250 km) per second.

REPEAT PERFORMANCE

The Sun, the Moon, and the Earth return to the same relative positions in space after a period of 18 years, 11 days. This period, called the saros, has been known since Babylonian times.

FLEETING SHADOW

During a solar eclipse, the Moon's shadow races across the Earth's surface at a speed of more than 1860 miles per hour.

THE END

In 5-6 billion years, the Sun will stop shining. By then it will have shrunk into a black dwarf star about the size of the Earth.

Words to Understand

asteroids
Lumps of rock that orbit the Sun in a band between the orbits of Mars and Jupiter.

astrology
A belief that people's lives are affected by the planets and the stars.

astronomers
Scientists who study the stars and space.

atmosphere
A layer of gases around a planet or a star.

aurora
A display of colored lights in far northern and far southern skies.

axis
An imaginary line around which a body spins.

calendar
A means of dividing up the year into months, weeks, and days.

chemical elements
The basic chemicals found in all kinds of substances; the building blocks of matter.

chromosphere
The Sun's colored inner atmosphere.

climate
The typical weather of a place during the year.

comet
An icy ball of matter that starts to glow when it nears the Sun.

constellation
A group of bright stars that appear in the same part of the sky.

corona
The white outer atmosphere of the Sun.

coronagraph
An instrument that shows the Sun's corona.

cosmic year
The time the Sun takes to travel once around the center of our galaxy

day
The time the Earth takes to spin round once in space.

eclipse
When one heavenly body passes in front of another and blocks its light.

ecliptic
The path the Sun seems to follow among the stars, as viewed from the Earth.

elements
see chemical elements

Equator
An imaginary line around the Earth, midway between the North and South Poles.

equinox
A time of the year when the hours of daylight and night-time are the same.

flare
A sudden outburst of energy on the Sun.

fusion
A process in which atoms join together.

galaxy
A great star "island" in space, containing many billions of stars.

gravity
The force that attracts one lump of matter to another.

leap year
A year 366 days long, one day more than the ordinary calendar year.

light-year
A unit astronomers use to measure distances in space. It eauals the distance light travels in a year—about 93 million miles.

moon
A natural satellite of a planet.

nuclear reaction
A process that involves the nuclei (centers) of atoms. Nuclear fusion is a reaction in which the nuclei of atoms join together.

orbit
The path in space a body follows when it circles around another.

ozone layer
A layer of a gas called ozone, found high in the Earth's atmosphere.

photosphere
The bright outer surface of the Sun.

photosynthesis
The process green plants use to make their food in daylight.

planet
A large body that circles in space around the Sun.

prominence
A fountain of flaming gas that rises through the Sun's atmosphere.

satellite
A body or an object that circles around another body in space. The Moon is a natural satellite of the Earth. The Earth also has many artificial satellites.

season
A period of the year when temperatures and the weather are much the same as in previous years.

solar
To do with the Sun.

solar cell
An electronic device that changes sunlight directly into electricity.

solar eclipse
An eclipse of the Sun.

Solar System
The Sun's family which includes the planets and their moons, asteroids, and comets.

solar wind
A stream of particles given out by the Sun.

spectrum
A spread of colors created when sunlight passes through a prism, or wedge of glass.

star
A huge ball of hot gases, which gives off energy as light, heat, and other radiation.

sundial
A device that measures the time when the Sun is out by the position of the shadow of a pointer on a dial.

sunspot
A dark patch on the Sun's surface.

total eclipse
The moment during an eclipse of the Sun when the Moon totally covers the Sun and makes the sky dark.

Universe
Everything that exists—the Earth, space, stars, and planets.

year
The time the Earth takes to circle once in space around the Sun.

zodiac
An imaginary band in the heavens in which the Sun and the planets are found.

Index